KINGFISHER READERS

Minibeasts

Anita Ganeri

First published 2012 by Kingfisher
an imprint of Macmillan Children's Books
a division of Macmillan Publishers Limited
20 New Wharf Road, London N1 9RR
Basingstoke and Oxford
Associated companies throughout the world
www.panmacmillan.com

Series editor: Heather Morris
Literacy consultant: Hilary Horton

ISBN: 978-0-7534-3093-4

9 8 7 6 5 4 3 2 1

1TR/1011/WKT/UNTD/105MA

A CIP catalogue record for this book is available from the British Library.

Printed in China

Picture credits
The Publisher would like to thank the following for permission to reproduce their material. Every care has been taken to trace copyright holders. However, if there have been unintentional omissions or failure to trace copyright holders, we apologize and will, if informed, endeavour to make corrections in any future edition.
Top = t; Bottom = b; Centre = c; Left = l; Right = r
Cover Shutterstock/Vaclav Volrab; Pages 6 Naturepl/Philippe Clement; 7 Frank Lane Picture Agency(FLPA)/Paul Hobson; 8 Shutterstock/Daniel Prudeck; 9 Shutterstock/teekaygee; 10bl Science Photo Library/Dr John Brackenbury; 10bc Shutterstock/Peter Waters; 11t Ardea/John Clegg; 11b Ardea/Steve Hopkin; 12 Shutterstock/VasilyVishnevskiy; 14 Shutterstock/orionmystery@flickr; 15t FLPA/Treat Davidson; 15b Shutterstock/Cathy Keifer; 16 Shutterstock/Alexey Filatov; 17t Shutterstock/2happy; 17b Shutterstock/Evgeniy Ayupov; 20 Naturepl/Kim Taylor; 21t Naturepl/Nick Upton; 21b Shutterstock/orionmystery@flickr; 23 Naturepl/Hans Christoph Kappel; 24 Shutterstock/Cathy Keifer; 25t Naturepl/Stephen Dalton; 25b Naturepl/Kim Taylor; 26 FLPA/Thomas Marent/Minden; 27t Ardea/Ian Beames; 27b Shutterstock/Platsee; 28 FLPA/Pete Oxford/Minden.

Contents

What are minibeasts?

Minibeasts are small animals. You can also call them creepy-crawlies. **Insects** such as ants, wasps, butterflies and beetles are minibeasts.

Insects are not the only minibeasts. Spiders, slugs and snails are also minibeasts. Woodlice, **leeches** and **centipedes** are minibeasts, too.

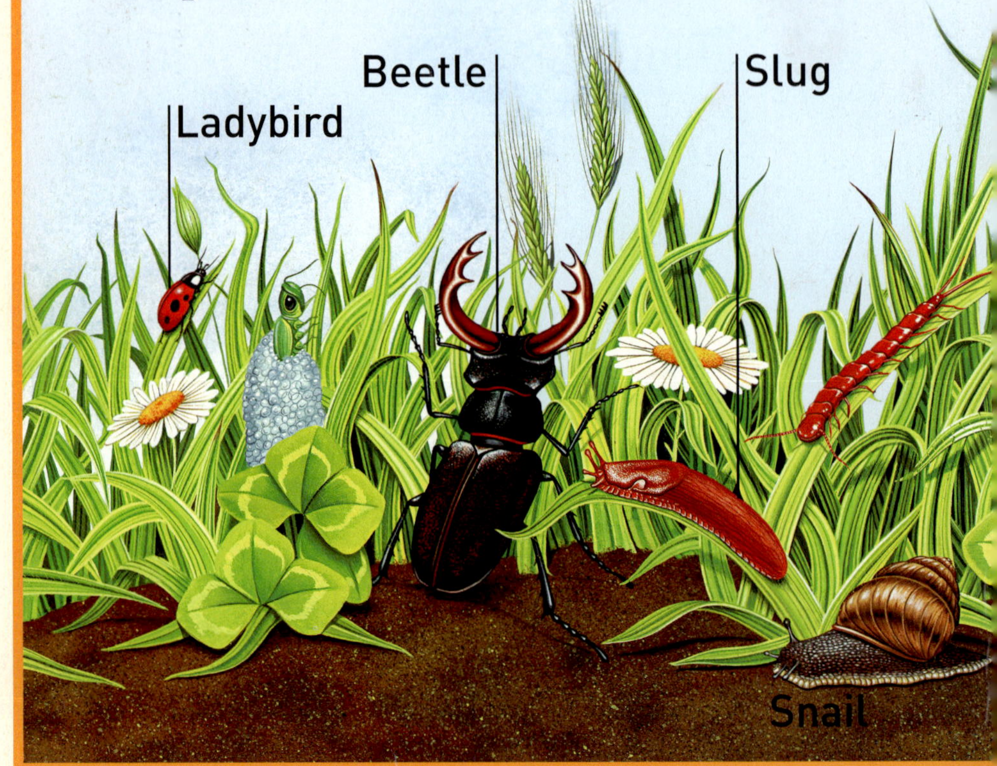

Some minibeasts live on land, and some live in ponds, rivers and the sea.

Did you know?
There are more than a million kinds of insects. That's more than any other kind of animal!

Where do minibeasts live?

Minibeasts live almost everywhere. You can find lots in gardens and parks. Watch butterflies feeding on flowers. Turn over a stone to find a woodlouse. Look out for webs on fences or outside windows. Spiders make these webs.

Did you know?
Earthworms are minibeasts that live underground.

Minibeasts also live in fields, woods, rivers and ponds. A pond is a good place to see minibeasts. A dragonfly has very long wings for flying fast across the water. It catches other insects to eat. Some types of spiders, snails and beetles live under the water.

Minibeast bodies

This minibeast is a honeybee. A honeybee is a kind of insect. Every insect has three pairs of legs (that's six legs altogether). Most insects have wings and can fly. An insect has a hard case around its body.

This minibeast is a spider. A spider has eight legs, not six like an insect. Most spiders have two rows of four eyes (that's eight eyes altogether).

Did you know?
Millipedes have lots more legs than insects or spiders. Some millipedes have 375 pairs of legs – that's 750 legs altogether!

How do minibeasts move?

Minibeasts move in different ways. They fly, hop, crawl or **slither** using their wings, long legs and slippery bodies. A grasshopper has long back legs for jumping. It can leap high in the air. When it is high enough, it opens its wings and flies. Grasshoppers jump to get away from hungry birds.

Did you know?
A honeybee flaps its wings about 250 times a second to stay up in the air.

A water boatman is an insect that lives in ponds. It lies on its back in the water. Then it uses its back legs to row along. It chases after **tadpoles** and small fish that it catches and eats.

Did you know?
Slugs and snails leave slimy trails behind them. The slime helps them to slide across the ground.

Minibeast travels

Some minibeasts don't travel very far. They crawl up a plant stem, or fly from tree to tree. But monarch butterflies are amazing. They live in Canada in summer, then in winter they fly south all the way to California or to Mexico where it is warm. This is more than 3,000 kilometres.

Every year, millions of globe-skimmer dragonflies make an even longer journey. They fly high in the sky and **glide** on the wind across the sea from India to Africa.

Did you know?
Some birds follow the dragonflies as they fly, and eat them!

Did you know?
The butterflies fly to the same place every year. Sometimes they even find the same trees.

Minibeast senses

Minibeasts use their senses to find out about the world around them. A fly has two huge eyes on the sides of its head. Each eye has hundreds of tiny **lenses**. The insect uses its eyes to see tiny movements.

Did you know?
A cricket has ears on its front legs. They are tiny holes with skin stretched across the top.

Insects use **antennae** for smelling. A male moth has long antennae that look like feathers. It can pick up smells from a long way away. Insects also use their antennae for tasting and touching things.

Did you know?
Spiders can't see very well. They use the hairs on their bodies to help them find their way.

What minibeasts eat

Minibeasts eat many different things. Leeches are minibeasts that feed on blood. A leech has a sucker at each end of its body. It sticks on to an animal, then starts to drink. When the leech is full it falls off.

Bees visit flowers to drink **nectar** and collect **pollen**. The bee brushes the yellow, powdery pollen into little baskets on its back legs. When these are full the bee flies to its nest and feeds the pollen to its young.

Did you know?
Cockroaches aren't fussy eaters. They eat almost anything, from plants to the rubbish you throw in the bin.

Although many minibeasts eat leaves, stems, flowers and pollen, others eat meat, blood and each other!

This mantis is eating a spider.

Butterfly life story

A butterfly starts life as a tiny egg, but it grows up quickly. Here is its life story.

1. In the spring, a female butterfly lays some eggs on a leaf.
2. The eggs hatch and a **caterpillar** wriggles out of each egg.
3. The caterpillars eat the leaves and grow bigger and bigger.

Did you know?
A female butterfly can lay 100 eggs every day!

4. Then each caterpillar makes a hard case around its body. The case is called a **chrysalis**.

5. Inside the case, the caterpillar's body turns into a butterfly.

6. The chrysalis splits open and the butterfly wriggles out. Its wings are soft and wet. They dry in the sun.

7. Then the butterfly flies away.

Minibeast mothers

Most minibeasts lay eggs then leave them, but a mother earwig looks after her eggs. She lays them in a hole in the ground and washes them to keep them clean. If an egg rolls away, she pulls it back again to keep it safe.

Did you know?
A cuckoo bee doesn't look after her eggs. She lays them in another bee's nest.

A female wolf spider lays her eggs inside a ball of silk. She carries the ball around with her as she hunts for insects to eat. When the baby spiders hatch, they climb on to their mother's back.

Minibeast builders

Some minibeasts build nests where they lay their eggs. Others build webs and traps to catch food. Honeybees build a nest called a **hive** in a hole in a tree. Inside, they make rows of tiny boxes, or cells, out of **wax**. The bees store honey and lay eggs in the cells.

A trapdoor spider lives in a burrow under the ground. The **burrow** has a door that can open and shut. The spider sits by the door and waits for an insect to pass by. Then the spider opens the door, jumps on the insect and eats it.

Did you know?
Termites are tiny insects that build enormous mud nests. Some termite towers are three times taller than a tall person.

Fangs and stings

Spiders eat insects and other minibeasts. Some spiders hunt for food. Others trap insects in their sticky webs. They use poison to kill the insects. The spider takes a bite and squirts in poison with its **fangs**.

A spider kills its trapped prey.

Did you know?
A bombardier beetle shoots a jet of hot poison at enemies. It fires the poison out of its tail. Bang!

Birds and other animals eat minibeasts. Wasps use poison to keep them away.
A wasp has a long, sharp sting at the end of its tail. It sticks its sting into an enemy and then squirts out poison.

Colours and patterns

Can you see this minibeast? It has a pink body and flaps that look like petals. It looks like a pink flower, but if a small insect lands on it, it gets a nasty shock. The flower is really a large insect called a mantis. The mantis grabs the insect and gobbles it up.

Did you know?
A hawkmoth has eyes on its wings. They're not real eyes but they look scary to birds.

Minibeasts use colours and patterns to hide from their enemies. One kind of leaf insect has a green body that is the same shape as a leaf. When it sits on a real leaf, it is very hard to see.

Hairy spider

Some minibeasts are not mini at all. This spider is called a bird-eater. It has a big, hairy body and long, hairy legs. It is one of the biggest spiders in the world and can grow as big as a large plate.

The bird-eater lives in a burrow and comes out at night to look for food. It eats insects and other spiders, but also catches **lizards** and small birds. It waits for them to come near, then grabs them and bites them.

Did you know?
If a bird-eater is scared, it hisses. Then it flicks hairs into its attacker's face.

Glossary

antennae Long stalks on an insect's head. They are used for smelling, tasting and touching.

burrow A hole a minibeast digs in the ground to live in or lay its eggs in.

caterpillar A small creature that hatches from the egg of a butterfly or moth.

centipede A long minibeast with lots of body sections and lots of legs.

chrysalis The hard case that a caterpillar makes around its body.

fang A special tooth that squirts poison as it bites.

glide To move through the air without flapping the wings.

hive A nest built by bees.

insect A minibeast with six legs and a hard case around its body.

leeches Minibeasts that drink other animals' blood.

lenses Clear discs in animals' eyes that help them to see.

lizard A type of reptile. Other reptiles include snakes, crocodiles and tortoises. All reptiles have scaly skin.

nectar A sweet liquid made inside flowers that many insects eat.

pollen A powder made inside flowers that helps in making seeds.

slither To move along by sliding.

tadpole A creature that hatches out of the egg of a frog or a toad.

termite A tiny creature that builds huge nests like towers.

wax A soft material that bees make and use to build nests.

Index